Contents:

PART 1

Uppercase and Lowercase Letters

Trace the letters and then practice writing the letters in the space to the right

A a Alphabet

A A A

A A A

A A A

A A A

A A A

A A A

a a a

a a a

a a a

a a a

a a a

B b Baby

B B B

B B B

B B B

B B B

B B B

B B B

b b b

b b b

b b b

b b b

b b b

C c Camel

C C C

C C C

C C C

C C C

C C C

C C C

c c c

c c c

c c c

c c c

c c c

D d Daytime

D D D

D D D

D D D

D D D

D D D

D D D

d d d

d d d

d d d

d d d

d d d

E e Excellent

E E E

E E E

E E E

E E E

E E E

E E E

e e e

e e e

e e e

e e e

e e e

Ff Favorite

F F F

F F F

F F F

F F F

F F F

F F F

f f f

f f f

f f f

f f f

f f f

G g Grimace

H h Health

H H H

H H H

H H H

H H H

H H H

H H H

h h h

h h h

h h h

h h h

h h h

I i Itchy

I I I

I I I

I I I

I I I

I I I

I I I

i i i

i i i

i i i

i i i

i i i

J j Juggle

Kk Karate

K K K

K K K

K K K

K K K

K K K

K K K

k k k

k k k

k k k

k k k

k k k

L l Legend

L L L

L L L

L L L

L L L

L L L

L L L

l l l

l l l

l l l

l l l

l l l

M m Manatee

M M M

M M M

M M M

M M M

M M M

M M M

m m m

m m m

m m m

m m m

m m m

N n Nanny

N N N

N N N

N N N

N N N

N N N

N N N

n n n

n n n

n n n

n n n

n n n

O o Oxygen

P p Papyrus

P P P

P P P

P P P

P P P

P P P

P P P

p p p

p p p

p p p

p p p

p p p

Q q Quaking

R r Ragweed

S s Saucers

T t Taxicab

T T T

T T T

T T T

T T T

T T T

T T T

t t t

t t t

t t t

t t t

t t t

U u Unwound

U U U

U U U

U U U

U U U

U U U

U U U

u u u

u u u

u u u

u u u

u u u

V v Vacuum

V V V

V V V

V V V

V V V

V V V

V V V

v v v

v v v

v v v

v v v

v v v

Ww Weather

W W W

W W W

W W W

W W W

W W W

W W W

w w w

w w w

w w w

w w w

w w w

X x Xylophone

X X X

X X X

X X X

X X X

X X X

X X X

x x x

x x x

x x x

x x x

x x x

Y y Yeast

PART 2

Trace and Practice Writing Words

Trace the letters and words and then practice writing the words on the line below

C i t i z e n s

Citizens Citizens

E l e c t i o n

Election Election

G o v e r n m e n t

Government Government

R e s o l u t i o n

Resolution Resolution

D u t i f u l

Dutiful Dutiful

J u s t i c e

Justice Justice

S i t u a t i o n

Situation Situation

D i m u n i t i o n

Dimunition Dimunition

C o n v i c t i o n

Conviction Conviction

H i t h e r t o

Hitherto Hitherto

I n c l i n a t i o n

Inclination Inclination

M o t i v e s

Motives Motives

U n a n i m o u s

Unanimous Unanimous

E n t i t l e d

Entitled Entitled

P a r t i a l i t y

Partiality Partiality

A d m i n i s t e r

Administer Administer

F a l l i b l e

Fallible Fallible

Q u a l i f i e d

Qualified Qualified

A d m o n i s h e s

Admonishes Admonishes

P a t r i o t i s m

Pastriotism Patriotism

P o l i t i c a l

Political Political

E x e r t i o n

Exertion Exertion

T e r m i n a t e

Terminate Terminate

B e l o v e d

Beloved Beloved

S t e a d f a s t

Steadfast Steadfast

M a n i f e s t i n g

Manifesting Manifesting

I n v i o l a b l e

Inviolable

A g i t a t e d

Agitated Agitated

D i s c o u r a g e d

Discouraged Discouraged

E s s e n t i a l

Essential Essential

P e n e t r a t e d

Penetrated Penetrated

U n c e a s i n g

Unceasing Unceasing

Z e a l

Zeal Zeal

Z e a l o u s

Zelaous Zealous

D u b i o u s

Dubious Dubious

S a c r e d l y

Sacredly Sacredly

W a r n i n g s

Warnings Warnings

A u s p i c e s

Auspices Auspices

I n t e r w o v e n

Interwoven Interwoven

Q u a r t e r s

Quarters Quarters

PART 3

Trace and Practice Writing Sentences

Trace the sentences and then practice writing the sentences in the space below

A was an ant

Who seldom stood still,

He made a very nice house

In the side of a hill.

A A

A A

a a a

a a a

B was a book
With a binding of blue
And pictures and stories
For me and for you.

B B B
B B B
b b b
b b b

C was a cat

Who ran after a rat

But his courage did fail

When she seized on his tail.

C C C

C C C

c c c

c c c

D was a dove,
Who lived in a wood,
With such pretty soft wings,
And so gentle and good!

D D D
D D D
d d d
d d d

E was an eagle,
Who sat on the rocks,
And looked down on the
And the far-away flocks.

E E E

E E E

e e e

e e e

F was a fan
Made of beautiful stuff;
And when it was used,
It went puffy-puff-puff!

F F F

F F F

f f f

f f f

G was a gooseberry,

Perfectly red;

To be made into jam,

And eaten with bread.

G G G

G G G

g g g

g g g

H was a heron,
Who stood in a stream:
The length of his neck
And his legs was extreme.

H H H
H H H
h h h
h h h

I was an inkstand,

Which stood on a table,

With a pen to write with

When we are able.

I I I

I I I

i i i

i i i

I was a jug,
So pretty and white,
With fresh water in it
At morning and night.
J J J
J J J
j j j
j j j

K was a kingfisher:

Quickly he flew,

So bright and so pretty!

Green, purple, and blue.

K K K

K K K

k k k

k k k

L was a lily,

So white and so sweet!

To see it and smell it

Was quite a nice treat.

L L L

L L L

l l l

l l l

M was a man,

Who walked all around;

And he wore a long coat

That reached the ground.

M M M

M M M

m m m

m m m

N was a nut

So smooth and so brown!

And when it was ripe,

It fell tumble-dum-down.

N N N

N N N

n n n

n n n

O was an oyster,

Who lived in his shell:

If you let him alone,

He felt perfectly well.

O O O

O O O

o o o

o o o

P was a polly,
All red, blue, and green,
The most beautiful polly
That ever was seen.

P P P

P P P

p p p

p p p

Q was a quill

Made into a pen;

But I do not know where,

And I cannot say when.

Q Q Q

Q Q Q

q q q

q q q

R was a rattlesnake,
Rolled up so tight,
Those who saw him ran
For fear he should bite.

R R R

R R R

r r r

r r r

S was a screw
To screw down a box;
And then it was fastened
Without any locks.

S S S
S S S
s s s
s s s

T was a thimble,
Of silver so bright!
When placed on the finger,
It fitted so tight!

T T T
T T T
t t t
t t t

Ut was an upper coat,
Woolly and warm,
To wear over all
In the snow or the storm.

U U U
U U U
u u u
u u u

V was a veil
With a border upon it,
And a ribbon to tie it
All round a pink bonnet.

V V V
V V V
v v v
v v v

W was a watch,

Where, in letters of gold,

The hour of the day

You might always behold.

W W W

W W W

w w w

w w w

X was King Xerxes,

Who wore on his head

A mighty large turban,

Green, yellow, and red.

X X X

X X X

x x x

x x x

Y was a yak,
From the land of Thibet:
Except his white tail,
He was all black as jet.

Y Y Y
Y Y Y
y y y
y y y

Z was a zebra,

Striped white and black;

And if he were tame,

You might ride on his back.

Z Z Z

Z Z Z

z z z

z z z

PART 4

Trace and Practice Writing Paragraphs

Trace the paragraph and then practice writing the paragraph in the space below

The Bat and the Weasels

A bat who fell upon the ground and was caught by a Weasel pleaded to be spared his life. The Weasel refused, saying that he was by nature the enemy of all birds. The Bat assured him that he was not a bird, but a mouse, and thus was set free. Shortly afterwards the Bat again fell to the ground and was caught by another Weasel, whom he likewise entreated not to eat him. The Weasel said that he had a special hostility to mice. The Bat assured him that he was not a mouse, but a bat, and thus a second time escaped.

Moral: It is wise to turn circumstances to good account.

The Wolf and the Crane

A wolf who had a bone stuck in his throat hired a Crane, for a large sum, to put her head into his mouth and draw out the bone. When the Crane had extracted the bone and demanded the promised payment, the Wolf, grinning and grinding his teeth, exclaimed: "Why, you have surely already had a sufficient recompense, in having been permitted to draw out your head in safety from the mouth and jaws of a wolf."

Moral: In serving the wicked, expect no reward, and be thankful if you escape injury for your pains.

The Hare and the Tortoise

A Hare one day ridiculed the short feet and slow pace of the Tortoise, who replied, laughing: "Though you be swift as the wind, I will beat you in a race." The Hare, believing her assertion to be quite simply impossible, assented to the proposal; and they agreed that the Fox should choose the course and fix the goal. On the day appointed for the race the two started together. The Tortoise never for a moment stopped, but went on with a slow but steady pace straight to the end of the course. The Hare, lying down by the wayside, fell fast asleep. At last waking up, and moving as fast as he could, he saw the Tortoise had reached the goal.

Moral: Slow but steady wins the race.

The Flies and the Honey-Pot

A number of Flies were attracted to a jar of honey which had been overturned in a housekeeper's room, and placing their feet in it, ate greedily.

Their feet, however, became so smeared with the honey that they could not use their wings, nor release themselves, and were suffocated.

Just as they were expiring, they exclaimed, "O foolish creatures that we are, for the sake of a little pleasure we have destroyed ourselves."

Moral: Pleasure bought with pains, hurts.

The Man and the Lion

A Man and a Lion traveled together through the forest. They soon began to boast of their respective superiority to each other in strength and prowess. As they were disputing, they passed a statue carved in stone, which represented "a Lion strangled by a Man." The traveler pointed to it and said: "See there! How strong we are, and how we prevail over even the king of beasts."

The Lion replied: "This statue was made by one of you men. If we Lions knew how to erect statues, you would see the Man placed under the paw of the Lion."

Moral: One story is good, till another is told.

The Fox and the Goat

A Fox one day fell into a deep well and could find no means of escape. A Goat, overcome with thirst, came to the same well, and seeing the Fox, inquired if the water was good.

Concealing his sad plight under a merry guise, the Fox indulged in a lavish praise of the water, saying it was excellent beyond measure, and encouraged him to descend. The Goat, mindful only of his thirst, thoughtlessly jumped down, but just as he drank, the Fox informed him of the difficulty they were both in and suggested a scheme for their common escape. "If," said he, "you will place your feet upon the wall and bend your head, I will run up your back and escape, and will help you out afterwards." The Goat readily assented and the Fox leaped upon his back. Steadying himself with the Goat's horns, he safely reached the mouth of the well and made off as fast as he could.

When the Goat upbraided him for breaking his promise, he turned around and cried out, "You foolish old fellow! If you had as many brains in your head as you have hairs in your beard, you would never have gone down before you had inspected the way up, nor have exposed yourself to dangers from which you had no means of escape."

Moral: Look before you leap.

BONUS

Additional Blank Pages to Practice your Handwriting

Blank Pages to Practice your Handwriting

www.ingramcontent.com/pod-product-compliance
Lightning Source LLC
Chambersburg PA
CBHW081418250726
48654CB00013B/1740

9798676703660